Opossums

by JoAnn Early Macken

Reading consultant: Susan Nations, M.Ed.,
author/literacy coach/consultant

WR WEEKLY READER

EARLY LEARNING LIBRARY

Please visit our web site at: www.earlyliteracy.cc
For a free color catalog describing Weekly Reader® Early Learning Library's list of high-quality books, call 1-877-445-5824 (USA) or 1-800-387-3178 (Canada). Weekly Reader® Early Learning Library's fax: (414) 336-0164.

Library of Congress Cataloging-in-Publication Data

Macken, JoAnn Early, 1953–
    Opossums / JoAnn Early Macken.
      p. cm. — (Animals that live in the forest)
    Includes bibliographical references and index.
    ISBN 0-8368-4483-1 (lib. bdg.)
    ISBN 0-8368-4490-4 (softcover)
    1. Opossums—Juvenile literature. I. Title.
  QL737.M34M34   2005
  599.2'76—dc22   2004057210

This edition first published in 2005 by
Weekly Reader® Early Learning Library
330 West Olive Street, Suite 100
Milwaukee, WI 53212 USA

Copyright © 2005 by Weekly Reader® Early Learning Library

Art direction: Tammy West
Cover design and page layout: Kami Koenig
Picture research: Diane Laska-Swanke

Picture credits: Cover, © James P. Rowan; p. 5 © Gary Meszaros/
Visuals Unlimited; pp. 7, 11 © Alan & Sandy Carey; pp. 9, 13, 21 © Steve
Maslowski/Visuals Unlimited; pp. 15, 17 © Michael H. Francis; p. 19
© William Grenfell/Visuals Unlimited

Printed in the United States of America

1 2 3 4 5 6 7 8 9 09 08 07 06 05

Note to Educators and Parents

Reading is such an exciting adventure for young children! They are beginning to integrate their oral language skills with written language. To encourage children along the path to early literacy, books must be colorful, engaging, and interesting; they should invite the young reader to explore both the print and the pictures.

Animals That Live in the Forest is a new series designed to help children read about forest creatures. Each book describes a different forest animal's life cycle, eating habits, home, and behavior.

Each book is specially designed to support the young reader in the reading process. The familiar topics are appealing to young children and invite them to read — and re-read — again and again. The full-color photographs and enhanced text further support the student during the reading process.

In addition to serving as wonderful picture books in schools, libraries, homes, and other places where children learn to love reading, these books are specifically intended to be read within an instructional guided reading group. This small group setting allows beginning readers to work with a fluent adult model as they make meaning from the text. After children develop fluency with the text and content, the book can be read independently. Children and adults alike will find these books supportive, engaging, and fun!

— Susan Nations, M.Ed., author, literacy coach,
and consultant in literacy development

A baby opossum climbs into its mother's **pouch**. The pouch is like a pocket. It may hold a dozen tiny babies. They have no hair. They cannot see or hear.

5

The babies drink milk
from their mother.
After about two
months, they open their
eyes. They look out at
the world. They crawl
out of the pouch.

The babies stay near their mother. She shows them how to find food and climb trees. She carries them on her back.

Opossums have long noses and tails. They also have whiskers and lots of teeth. Their fur is gray and white.

Opossums live near water.
They are good climbers.
They can hold onto
branches with their tails.
Babies can even hang
by their tails!

Opossums sniff to find their food. They eat grass and fruit. They eat eggs, insects, and small animals.

During the day, they sleep in dens. A den may be in an old log or tree stump. It may be an old den from another animal.

An opossum in danger
may stop moving.
Other animals think it
is dead. They leave
it alone.

Opossums are awake at night. They hunt for food. They climb trees to escape from danger. Opossums are at home in the forest.

Glossary

dens — places where wild animals rest or live

newborn — just born

pouch — a part of an animal's body that is like a pocket

sniff — to try to smell something by breathing in

whiskers — long, bristly hair on an animal's face

For More Information

Books

Opossum. Wild America (series). Lee Jacobs (Blackbirch Press)

Opossum at Sycamore Road. Smithsonian's Backyard (series). Sally M. Walker (Smithsonian Books)

Opossums. Sandra Lee (Child's World)

Opossums. What's Awake (series). Patricia Whitehouse (Heinemann)

Web Sites

Virginia Opossum
www.iwrc-online.org/kids/Facts/Mammals/ opossum.htm
Opossum facts and pictures from the International Wildlife Rehabilitation Council

23

Index

About the Author

JoAnn Early Macken is the author of two rhyming picture books, *Sing-Along Song* and *Cats on Judy*, and six other series of nonfiction books for beginning readers. Her poems have appeared in several children's magazines. A graduate of the M.F.A. in Writing for Children and Young Adults program at Vermont College, she lives in Wisconsin with her husband and their two sons. Visit her Web site at www.joannmacken.com.

24